To a's
Live and Let G
You are Powerful

DEPRESSION

7 Ways to Live and Let Go

by

Taurea Vision Avant

ISBN-13: 978-0991298433

ISBN-10: 0991298438

Dedication

I want to first thank you so much for supporting this book. It definitely took a lot for me to first come out and tell people that I was depressed and then to make a decision to write about it and share my story, the stories of others, and steps to getting through this emotional disease. I would like to dedicate this book to the beautiful Jessica Thomas, who truly was the motivator for me deciding to write this book. I released a video in early 2015, and while I received so many messages, it was Jessica who really motivated me to put together a book that I know can impact so many people.

I would also like to give a special dedication to those that are going through depression or that have lost their lives to depression. Depression is an emotional disease that can truly cause so many physical complications in the body, from heart disease to cancers and more. I watched my mother allow depression to overtake her from alcoholism, and when my dad was diagnosed with cancer, I saw depression speed up his disease and completely turn him into someone I couldn't even recognize.

Table of Contents

Acknowledgements

I have to acknowledge some very special people in my life who were there for me during my troubled times. I first want to acknowledge Veronica Terry, my mother. She was sent to me at a point in my life when I was going through the changes of life, changing from a child to a woman. While God called my biological mother home at a young age, he sent a woman who I have been able to confide in and love with all my heart. You have been a true blessing.

I also would like to acknowledge First Lady Michelle and Pastor Karol Warren of Hebron Church, who have played a major role in my life as well. They are my parents sent to me from God to watch after me and to keep me close to God. I have to also make sure that I send love to my photographer, Jay Douglas (IG @vodphoto) of www.VodPhoto.com, who did such an incredible job with this cover, along with Eboni Hall (IG @ebonisierramua) ,who blessed me with incredible makeup. Finally, there were some incredible individuals who actually participated in pre-ordering this book as well as contributing their stories about themselves or someone they knew that went through depression. Without these incredible supporters, I know that this book would not have grown to become the book that it is, and I know that it will absolutely impact so many people. I appreciate all who pre-ordered and those who have supported and bought this book. Here are the names of my pre-order supporters. Please reach out to them and let them know I sent you and that I am so grateful for them!

· **Angie Renee'**
www.angierenee.com
Author, Mentor, Speaker, Screenwriter, Activist

· **Carlos L. Brown**
Facebook.com/SuccessfulLos
Owner of Carlos And Sons HVAC Plus

· **Dione Mostella**
www.divalistic.com
Facebook.com/divalistictees
Owner of DivaListic Tees LLC

· **Desiree Pritchard**

· **Elaine Trimble**
www.EssentialsToHealthyLiving.com
Facebook.com/EssentialsToHealthyLiving
Owner of Essentials To Healthy Living

DEPRESSION ~ Live & Let Go!

· **Elissa Mitchell**
www.Marykay.com/emitchell9175
Facebook.com/Elissa.Mitchell.73
Independent Beauty Consultant

· **James & Natasha Roach**
www.MrandMrsRoach.com
Facebook.com/MRMRSroach
Owners of M & MR Marketing

· **Jerry Ross**

· **Kelli Skinner**

· **Kim Eliopoulos**
www.kimecafe.com
Business Owner

· **LaWonda Petty**
Facebook.com/Lawonda.Petty
Coffee Consultant

· **Marcia Rose**

· **Michael Brown**
Facebook.com/CellPhoneConcierge
Technical Creative Director/ Mobile Tech Consultant

DEPRESSION ~ Live & Let Go!

- **Sheree Ho-Shing**
Facebook.com/SFASpecialPlace
Organo Consultant

- **TaVona Denise**
TaVonaDenise.com
Facebook.com/Tavona
Business Accelerator and Success Coach

- **Tracee Randall**
TraceeRandall.com
Facebook.com/Tracee.S.Randall
Owner of Generational Health & Voice Coach

- **Troy "DJ Vex" Conway**
Facebook.com/djvex
Business Owner, DJ, Producer

Introduction

So why did I decide to write a book about depression? I know some may be asking that, especially if you are one who follows me on social media, because from the outside looking in, it may seem like I really don't have too many challenges. Side note: If you are not following me on social media, WHY ARE YOU NOT? Lol, Just playing...but no, I' not; go follow me. My social media handle is @VisionAvant. Okay, so back to the story...why would I write about depression? Well, you know, even though it may look as if I don't ever cry or have any challenges, the truth is I just choose not to show those days on social media. I am very careful with what it is that I put out there on the web, especially since I am seen as a "leader." However, I had a big wakeup call when one day someone reached out to me to tell me what they were going through—how they didn't want to live and that they felt like they could never live up to the kind of life that I had obtained. In my mind, I am like, "They have no idea." So I went to sleep with this beautiful woman's confession on my heart and in my head. The next day I then watched this movie of a young boy who felt all his life that he was born in the wrong kind of body. He felt that he was supposed to be a woman. So as a young child, he started dressing as a girl. Long story short, he also fell into a deep depression and ended up doing a video sharing his testimony and how he wanted to die. He didn't believe he had a place here in this world. It broke my heart because it was based off a true story. In the end, he didn't kill himself, and he also found love. It's such a great story. I just can't remember the name of it. I know, I know, I'm sorry. So it got me to thinking. You know, sometimes from the outside looking in, everything does look great. The unfortunate thing about that is that people will also compare their lives, thinking they can't really relate to you. I'm not saying it is good to compare yourself to others, but let's be honest, we do it. So I woke up on a Wednesday and decided that it was time to tell the world what I had been going through and that, no, my life isn't perfect. I shot a short video completely opening my life, with some restraint of course, to the world. I told them what I had been dealing with emotionally. I shared how I lost my parents at a young age, had my heart broken, lost a close friend, lost my income, lost my grandma, and pretty much lost my mind. I couldn't believe the response that I received from this video. I thought that would be the end of it; however, how many of you know that it's never the end of it? So I started to get so many emails, messages, text messages, tweets, etc., from people that were going through depression as well. I had so many people that I never imagined in my life would be going through depression who were going through it. I had women, men, white, black, young, old, and all other categories reaching out. It was truly, for me, one of the biggest blessings to know that sharing my testimony opened up a lot of people to share theirs as well. I even heard through the grapevine that there were some people who didn't necessarily appreciate the video and the timing, but guess what? My video wasn't for them. My video was for me and those that could also be released from the chains of depression—the guilt, the hurt, the anger, and all the other emotions that you go through when you are in this emotional state. When you think about it, Jesus wasn't appreciated as well by those that saw his works. Now, I am in no way comparing myself to the almighty Jesus, but what I am saying is that if a man who had no sin, who loved all, and who did great works was also condemned, then I must be doing something right. So I really don't care about those who had a problem with it. That's the problem with us today. We care too much about what someone else will say about choices that we make when not one of them is any better than us. THERE ARE NO PERFECT HUMANS IN THIS WORLD—PERIOD! Okay, let me calm down, lol, he is still working on me. I get a bit emotional when I am passionate about something.

Okay, so back to this depression. There would be days when I wouldn't get out of bed. There were days when I would literally drink two bottles of wine trying to drown my sorrows. By the way, my mother died of alcoholism, so that much wine was not a good look. Oh, if you are wondering, yes, I do still drink a glass a day, but it's for pleasure and not to hide. Anywho, I wasn't getting out of bed. I was feeling so sorry for myself, like nobody really cared about me. I mean, my biological mom and dad were gone. My grandma was gone, and just a month before she passed, I was telling her that I was going to come and spend time with her, and I hadn't. I felt like my friendships were failing and my ultimate "love of my life"—so I thought—totally threw me for a loop by getting engaged to a woman he barely knew. I just felt like I had hit rock bottom, and honestly, I didn't want to live anymore. I also felt like if I were to leave, I may be missed for a couple of days, but ultimately, everyone's life would go on. I even started researching how to commit suicide. My company had a major convention in Las Vegas, and I bought a bottle of sleeping pills and was ready to leave this world. The only thing that kept me from trying was the fact that after researching suicide, the chances of sleeping pills working was lower than 10%, and I don't like to do anything I can't succeed at. So I know this is a bit deep, but I truly want you to know all that I was dealing with. I remember one day my best friend, whom, by the way, I know was also a tremendous blessing to me because she really took care of me, finally spoke up to tell me that I needed to get out of bed. Monica Wilkerson is my best friend, and she is generally a very passive woman. She doesn't really like a lot of conflict, and I can be a firecracker at times, especially when I may disagree. Hey, don't judge. I'm just telling you the truth. However, when she told me that, I knew that I needed to do something. At the time, I tried to reach out to people whom I thought could help me. I would sit at church crying my eyes out. I would try to speak positive affirmations, but nothing was working—until I decided to join a small group at my church. I attend a church here in Atlanta called Buckhead Church, and while they may never ever truly know it, it was my small group that literally saved my life.

I joined this group of people that I didn't know, and we had a chance to study the Word of God. I had a chance to be around people who had no judgment because they really didn't know me. I never even told them I was

19

recently ready to commit suicide, but it wasn't really needed. I can't explain exactly why this particular group did it for me. I will say that they were most definitely the stepping stone to my recovery.

I then decided to get myself out of bed more and wake up smiling. I dove deeper into the Word, and my life started to feel better. Now I will tell you this, because of my emotional challenges, there were areas in my life that did suffer, but because I know that this is all a part of the journey, I still wake up grateful that he pulled me through. I AM ALIVE, so that means there is some living to do! You know, when I was going through this emotional sickness, which, by the way, I still every now and then have relapses with, I honestly was really only thinking of myself. I really didn't think about those who would be affected if I was gone. I convinced myself to believe that there was nobody, but there were hundreds who would be affected. When I live out my legacy, there will be millions.

The key is to know what you need to do to get back to the right state. Ultimately, we are in control of our emotions. It's one of the ultimate blessings that God gave us that we can choose who we want to be on any given day. Happy or sad, we are in control. So with that said, because of the responses that I received when I put out that video, I was given the idea by an incredible woman named Jessica Thomas, whom I dedicated this book to, to write this book. I really hope that you enjoy this book and that you share it with someone else that may need it. So with that said, let's get to it! It's time to live and let go!

By the way...before each chapter, I am going to include some Bible verses that I believe will also be a great asset to helping anyone through depression. I hope you enjoy them. I encourage you to go look up the verses and read the chapters in depth as well.

Chapter 1 : Who Is This Book For?

"But you, O LORD, are a shield about me, my glory, and the lifter of my head." (Psalm 3:3 ESV)

I wanted to include a chapter to really talk about who can truly benfit from this book only because even with me telling the world of my experiences with depression, I still know that a lot of my followers are not as comfortable with admitting that they may be or know someone that may be suffering from this horrible disease. I want you to know that this book is NOT JUST FOR THOSE SUFFERING from depression but also for those that are not sure if they are experiencing depression, and, more important, even those that have loved ones going through depression. I purposely made this book pretty simple to read but detailed enough so you can take action. I promise you, most have finished this book in less than a few days.

When you read this book, you may want to read it fully through and then identify the chapter(s) that is(are) most valuable to you and start acting upon it. I also have a great questionnaire that you can follow through to see where your mental state is. Go to www.TaureaAvant.com/depression. For those that have never experienced symptoms of depression, I want you know that you are truly blessed, and it could potentially be a blessing for you to connect with those that may be dealing with these challenges. I believe that positive energy is contagious and can help others. So once you learn how to help someone with depression, use your testimony of happiness to bless someone else. Also, once you have finished the book, please don't hesitate to share with me your thoughts and leave your rating of this book. The better the rating, the better we reach more and more people all over the world. This is a movement here, and I am just so grateful that you are a part of it.

Chapter 2: Depression

"It is the LORD who goes before you. He will be with you; he will not leave you or forsake you. Do not fear or be dismayed." (Deuteronomy 31:8 ESV)

What Is Depression?

Depression is something that has been around for thousands of years. WebMD uses the following words in its definition of depression: *"Major depression is an episode of sadness or apathy along with other symptoms that lasts at least two consecutive weeks and is severe enough to interrupt daily activities."*

According to Oxford Dictionaries, "Depression is feelings of severe despondency and dejection where self-doubt creeps in and swiftly turns to depression." It is a mental condition characterized by feelings of severe despondency and dejection, typically also with feelings of inadequacy and guilt and often accompanied by lack of energy and disturbance of appetite and sleep."

28

Now, if I were to be a dictionary, even though I am not, I would say depression for me is the state of not being happy and feeling sorry for yourself. In most cases when you are depressed, you are too hard on yourself and judging yourself for every little thing. You feel incomplete and that you don't want to be here anymore. You let your mistakes become bigger then what they really are. You feel everyone is judging you and that you just can't get things right. When you are depressed, you may be good at putting on a good face, but when you get home, the real you shows up, and you feel worthless. You often think that life would be better if you just gave up. Depressive thoughts begin to program your subconscious mind, which then programs

29

your conscious, which then creates your actions.

Symptoms of Depression

Now keep in mind that there are several different claims of symptoms of depression, and some can be more prominent in your life than others. I will first cover the symptoms according to WebMD.com, and then I will cover my personal symptoms that I dealt with. These are titled Taurea Avant Symptoms.

WebMD Symptoms

- Feelings of guilt, worthlessness, helplessness, or hopelessness
- Loss of interest or pleasure in usual activities, including sex
- Difficulty concentrating and complaints of poor memory

- Insomnia or oversleeping
- Appetite changes, which may include weight gain or loss
- Fatigue, lack of energy
- Thoughts of suicide or death
- Slow speech, slow movements

Taurea Avant Symptoms

- Uninterested in anything
- Sadness and feeling of worthlessness
- Enjoyed being in the dark
- Discouraged to be around anyone
- Great at masking my emotions
- Dependent on substances to numb my pain
- Lack of energy
- Daily thoughts of suicide or death

If you are feeling any of these things, I want you to know that you are not alone. I have seriously prayed for you as you are reading this book right now, and I will only ask that you finish it to the end. I encourage you to do as I have done and find a group to join, share your testimony, and get out and get active in the world. Let me slow down because I will of course give you more specific things that you can do to get over this! I will say that regardless if you are dealing with it or not, I am just very happy you are reading this book.

Statistics About Depression

You know, what's just a bigger confirmation that we need to increase the awareness of this disease, is that it was really hard to find some recent statistics about depression. When I checked the CDC's website, their latest statistics were for 2010. This is why we must do more as a people to bring awareness to this disease. I truly believe depression is a main cause to a lot of these other causes of death, like cancer and heart challenges. Our thoughts are everything, and I believe if we are not in the right state emotionally, it kills our health.

When I tried to do my research on the statistics, all I would see is depression linked with other things as one of many symptoms. It's so sad that even our own society doesn't really like to talk about depression. They link depression with so many other things. Now, I will say in fact that yes, sometimes depression is caused by some other things beyond our emotions, which I do discuss in this book. However, I just really am so surprised that it's not that easy to find statistics just on depression alone. They have to be tied with anxiety, bipolar disease, and other things, which I guess I understand, but honestly, can we just talk about depression alone? Can we get down to speaking on the purple elephant in the room?

Now, I must say that these statistics are alarming; however, I want to say that they probably aren't even accurate. There are so many people right now that are dealing with this sickness, and most don't even know. However, I thought it would be powerful to show you the recorded stats on depression. In the next section, I am going to discuss why a lot of people don't tell others what they are dealing with. My goal is that when I do explain why, it will empower you or someone you know to actually come out. There are so many more of us dealing with this, and a real-life testimony is empowering.

Here are the statistics of those dealing with depression according to the Uplift non-profit organization that specializes in helping people with depression. I am sorry I can't really share too much about the source because, well, to be honest, I don't even know that they are in business anymore. However, stay close to what we are doing because it is my goal to really get better statistics as well as increase awareness. I pray they are still working on their mission to help with depression, but their website hasn't been updated, and these statistics are from 2005. However, these were the most detailed that I could find.

- Depressive disorders affect approximately 18.8 million American adults, or about 9.5% of the U.S. population, age 18 and older in a given year. This includes major depressive disorder, dysthymic disorder, and bipolar disorder.

- Everyone will at some time in their life be affected by depression—their own or someone else's—according to Australian government statistics. (Depression statistics in Australia are comparable to those of the U.S. and UK.)

- Preschoolers are the fastest-growing market for antidepressants. At least four percent of preschoolers—over a million—are clinically depressed.

- The rate of increase of depression among children is an astounding 23%

- Fifteen percent of the population of most developed countries suffers from severe depression.

- Thirty percent of women are depressed. Men's figures were previously thought to be half that of women, but new estimates are higher than previously thought.

- Fifty-four percent of people believe depression is a personal weakness.

- Forty-one percent of depressed women are too embarrassed to seek help.

- A full 80% of depressed people are not currently being treated.

- Ninety-two percent of depressed African-American males do not seek treatment.

- A total of 15% of depressed people will commit suicide.

- Depression will be the second largest killer after heart disease by 2020, and studies show depression is a contributory factor to fatal coronary disease. Depression results in more absenteeism than almost any other physical disorder and costs employers more than $51 billion per year in absenteeism and lost productivity, not including high medical and pharmaceutical bills.

I hope these statistics definitely opened your eyes to how serious this disease really is. It all made sense to me. When I look at my loved ones who passed away from either cancer or an addiction, they were all in a bad mental state. I've even heard that in a lot of cases of cancer, most patients that passed away were also dealing with a broken heart or some relationship challenges, which of course can affect your mental state. It is true that our minds are truly the most powerful things we own, and they can totally affect our health in a major way.

Why People Don't Come out and Get Help

When I released my video where I shared with all my followers the challenges of life that I was dealing with, I never realized how many people would actually reach back out to me. In fact, I had so many people that I never imagined would reach out to me to tell me that they could totally relate. I had more men than I expected as well, which was a real shocker. So it did get me to thinking why a lot of people don't actually come out about what they are dealing with, and I just want to say that for those of you that are secretly dealing with this illness, I totally understand. I actually came up with five reasons why I believe that people never tell others what they are going through. They all stem from fears. If you have not had a chance to read my book *FEAR – 10 ways to let go of your fears*, I would most definitely recommend grabbing a copy of it as well. To get your copy, simply go to www.TaureaAvant.com and visit the store.

1. **Fear of Rejection** – This was one of my biggest fears. I myself attempted to reach out to some people in my life that I thought would be able to help me, and it just seemed to me that they couldn't handle it. I took it as rejection. I think, though, what it really was, was that they just didn't know what to do. The great thing is that I actually have a section in

this book that will explain what a person can do for someone that they see going through this illness. I think this will be very helpful.

2.   **Fear of Being Judged** – The last thing I wanted to feel was judged. I didn't want to hear that I needed to pray. I WAS PRAYING. I didn't want someone to think I wasn't fit to lead as well because of it. I just didn't want to deal with that at all. So to keep from being judged (at least that's what I thought), I just didn't tell certain people. I was in this leadership position too, and I feared that if people knew, it could affect my income. "How could someone that is depressed lead me?" That's just what I used to think.

3. **Fear of Isolation** – We sometimes believe that if we do tell someone what we are going through, they won't understand, and in return, they will not include us in things. You know the opposite was that I actually ended up isolating myself. My friends would reach out to me, and I was just constantly telling them no. I remember, in fact, when I finally told one of my friends what I was going through, she was in complete shock. She thought I just didn't want to be around her. That wasn't the case at all.

4. **Fear of Loss** – I thought that if I did reveal this secret (which, by the way, wasn't a secret to everyone), I would lose everything I had. All in all, the truth is the

longer I stayed in this state, the worse things got in my life. My finances, my relationships, my health, and my spirit all suffered. So what I feared if I told others what I was going through was happening on its own. Also, I guess, in my own mind, I believed that if I didn't reveal what was going on, then I still had a bit of control. Once I gave up that knowledge, somehow, in my mind, I would lose more control. I know it doesn't make sense, but remember, we are talking about an emotional illness that allows us to make a lot of irrational choices.

5. Fear of Humiliation – I am pretty sure a lot of people just don't come out for the fact that they feel embarrassed to be in this position. I mean, think about it...if you are seen as a powerful person or a leader, you may be hesitant just because you feel that you will be embarrassed. Honestly, though, the only way you can ever be embarrassed is if you allow yourself to be embarrassed. In most cases, the fact that a person at a leadership level can admit to this mental disease can sometimes be more powerful than not admitting. The reason is because people think that when you hit a certain level of success, you have no challenges. Knowing that you do and that you were able to fight through or at least admit it can be so powerful. You'll find out that instead of being embarrassed, more people will now be able to relate to the fact that, yes, you are human with human emotions.

Chapter 3:
Causes of Depression

"For I am sure that neither death nor life, nor angels nor rulers, nor things present nor things to come, nor powers, nor height nor depth, nor anything else in all creation, will be able to separate us from the love of God in Christ Jesus our Lord." (Romans 8:38-39 ESV)

While I can't say that I can totally relate to all the reasons why depression is caused, I wanted to give you a great array of possible reasons, so if you are going through this illness or you know someone who is, you can maybe get an idea of what happened.

I am going to give you a total of 12 different reasons according to Health.com with a few more that I added in myself.

- **S.A.D.** – S.A.D. stands for Seasonal Affective Disorder. Less than 6% of the population actually has this challenge. It is basically the body reacting to the changes in the weather. Alfred Lewy, MD, professor of psychiatry at Oregon Health and Science University in Portland, believes that instead of waking and enjoying dawn, the body has a hard time adjusting, he says, which could be due to imbalances in brain chemistry and the hormone melatonin.

- **Smoking** – Smoking has long been known to align with depression. There are questions whether people smoke because they are depressed or are depressed because they smoke. However, people who are going through depression are highly more likely to take up smoking. The reason why it is believed to have some linked causes to depression is because of the chemical imbalance that smoking causes.

Nicotine does affect the neurotransmitter activity in the brain,

49

resulting in higher levels of dopamine and serotonin.

If you have ever noticed someone that does smoke, they may be affected by mood swings that come with withdrawal, and this is why depression is associated with smoking cessation. This is where the addiction to cigarettes comes into play.

I would just say avoid cigarettes, and this can help with balancing your brain chemicals.

• **Thyroid disease** – According to Thyroid.com, there is an estimated 20 million Americans with some form of thyroid disease. Up to 60 percent of those with thyroid disease are unaware of their condition. Women are five to eight times more likely than men to have thyroid problems.

When the thyroid, a butterfly-shaped gland in the neck, doesn't produce enough thyroid hormone, it's known as hypothyroidism, and depression is one of its symptoms. This hormone is multifunctional, but one of its main tasks is to act as a neurotransmitter and regulate serotonin levels.

Make sure that you go ahead and have a thyroid test, especially of you experience new depression symptoms— particularly along with cold sensitivity, constipation, and fatigue. Hypothyroidism is treatable with medication. However, make sure to pay attention to the medication because it may not help the depression to get better.

- **Not sleeping enough** – I know this was definitely the assistant to my depression. In 2007 there was study where they showed upsetting images to participants. Of the ones who were operating under less sleep, they experienced more brain activity than the ones who were better rested. These are said to be the same reactions as those of depressed patients.

Sleeping is what allows the brain cells to be replenished. If you don't sleep, the brain stops working well, and this could lead to depression.

- **Social Media Overload** – If you are going through any emotional challenges, the worst thing you could do is turn to social media. I swear some people will let social media run their lives.

In a 2010 study, researchers found that about 1.2% of people ages 16 to 51 spent an inordinate amount of time online and that they had a higher rate of moderate to severe depression. However, the researchers noted that it is not clear if Internet overuse leads to depression or if depressed people are more likely to use the Internet. Again, it is the same situation in regards to smoking, but I will say, be careful how much time you spend online.

There have actually been a number of studies that associate social media with depression, especially in teens and preteens. Social media has caused many to struggle with real-life human interaction and a lack of companionship, and they may have an unrealistic view of the world. Some experts even call it Facebook, Instagram, or Twitter depression.

Do this for me—if you are a social media lover, after you finish this book, spend seven days off social media totally, and then send me an email and let me know how you feel. Send me an email by going to my website, www.TaureaAvant.com. I really hope you do this!

- **TV Programs (especially the end)** – When you think of a television series or a movie that you absolutely loved and if you were really into it, it could trigger depression. I know this may sound crazy, but if you are like me, then you really get emotionally into the movies you watch. To me, if a movie can't move you emotionally, then it's not a good movie. I've become so good with visualization that sometimes I may go too far emotionally with a movie. You know what I mean—a sad movie can totally affect your mood for the entire day.

"A lot of people are easily swept up in a narrative, forgetting about real life and [their] own problems," says Emily Moyer-Gusé, Ph.D., assistant professor of communications at Ohio State University in Columbus.

To me, one of the best films of all time was *Avatar*. I think I've watched it more than 10 times. Every time I watch it, it's like I never watched it before. In 2009 some *Avatar* fans reported feeling depressed and even suicidal because the movie's fictional world wasn't real. Wow... Now, I didn't get depressed from it, but I can see how one could be upset with not being able to live in a world as beautiful as Avatars. The graphics in the movie were so amazingly put together that it truly seemed real.

•   **Environment** – Where you live most definitely can affect you. At the end of 2014, I made a decision to put my house on the market. I could no longer live in that house any more. For me, that house just didn't have the right energy. For some reason, that house would just cause me to feel tired, especially in my bedroom. If I were ever in my bedroom, all I wanted to do was lay down on the bed and just sleep.

Also when it comes to your environment, you can be affected by the people you are around. The beliefs that people have can affect you. Your environment isn't just about physical location like your home or office but the people you are around. I heard recently that more and more of our brothers and sisters are falling into depression and even committing suicide because of certain choices that they have made in the way they live their lives. The environments that they are or were in are what absolutely strengthened their negative emotional state. I would say if you feel that where you spend the most of your time is where you feel the worst, then you most definitely need to get yourself in an environment where you feel better—even if it means moving. Seriously, what's more important, your life or where you live or work? For me, I'd rather be happy than be somewhere I feel depressed.

- **Where You Live** – Where you live also closely aligns with your environment. That's why I almost put them together. However, there is a slight difference. Where you live could also align with what part of the world you live in.

While I personally love to live in the city, research has found that people living in urban settings do have a 39% higher risk of mood disorders than those in rural regions. A 2011 study in the journal *Nature* offers an explanation for this trend: City dwellers have more activity in the part of the brain that

59

regulates stress, and higher levels of stress could lead to psychotic disorders.

So if you are a city girl or guy, then I would recommend that you make sure you are doing the best you can to supplement your brain so that it can stay strong. That is one of the things I personally have worked on, from meditation to eating better. Of course, I will give you great ideas later in this book.

• **Food Choices** – Have you ever heard the saying "You are what you eat"? Well, it is a known fact that your diet can affect your emotions.

According to Everydayhealth.com, "long-term exposure to an unhealthy diet is a risk factor for depression, according to the findings of a 2014 study in the online journal PLoS One that looked at diet and depression in 3,663 people. What constituted an unhealthy diet, for purposes of the study, was one that was high in sugar and processed foods. 'One of the symptoms used to diagnose depression is change in appetite, so there certainly could be a link between diet and depression,' says Anil Malhotra, MD, director of psychiatric research at Zucker Hillside Hospital in Glen Oaks, N.Y."

When I sat down to really look at my diet, I realized that what I was putting into my body most definitely was not ideal. I lacked major nutrition. I was dehydrated and catching colds left and right. I started to work on eating greener and drinking more water and saw a difference.

Also, it is said that one important thing we may be lacking is more omega-3 fatty acids. These are vitamins found in salmon and vegetable oils. There was a study that found an association between eating less fish and an increase in depression in women. These fatty acids actually will regulate the neurotransmitters like serotonin, which most definitely explains the link to depression.

- **Poor Relationships** – This was what I believe absolutely started me on my road to depression. I felt like I was betrayed by someone I thought was my soul mate, and then I had lost one of my great friends to cancer and didn't even know she was sick. I guess she didn't feel she could come to me. This soul mate of mine had me thinking so many negative things about people in my life. I found myself really turning my back on a lot of people because I thought he was the one. I put so much on my heart because I truly started to believe that I wasn't a good person. I don't blame him either. I really don't. We all have our own battles, and I'm no different. I just know that I was influenced by this, and to identify that I was easily influenced did hurt my heart. Then my friend who passed from cancer...my God, this hurt like hell. All I could think about was our last conversation we had, where I was telling her that we need to focus on where we are going and not where were at. She had fallen into some challenges, and I just wanted her to know I had her back and that I didn't want her to always discuss what wasn't good in her life. I lost my love and I lost my friend. I felt like I didn't deserve to have either love or lasting friendships. In my mind, I couldn't, for whatever reason, make either work. I was in the worst emotional place I could have ever been at that point. I didn't really have strong relationships with my family either, which also started to weigh heavy on me, and I honestly felt like I had no one who cared about me. Then my grandma also got sick, and I started to blame myself for a lot. I would evaluate how much time I spent with her and how much time I was spending with my friends. I was so busy building this business and trying to keep my head above water that I wasn't even taking time to be with my family and friends. I felt like my relationships were honestly failing more and more because of the decisions I made. I didn't think I deserved to have friends or family that loved me. I hadn't been there for them the way I wanted them there for me. I honestly started to make up my own reality of my relationship status with others in my head.

I had to let these false feelings go and know that I was loved. I had to forgive myself and know that I was a good person. I will tell you more of what I did to do this for myself later on.

- **Financial Challenges** – This was another challenge that added to my depression. After dealing with the loss of so many loved ones in my life, it did affect me becoming depressed, but then, even worse, it affected my activity within my business, which ultimately affected my income to the point where my income had dropped to 30% of what I had been making for the past three years, which was so challenging for me. This, of course, made me feel worse, which caused me to fall deeper into depression. Literally, my financial challenges were a result of the depression, but they also caused me to go deeper into depression. I had a friend who I totally believe it was her financial challenges that ultimately caused her sickness to escalate because of the mental state she was in. Finances are affecting so many people and their relationships, health, and more! Not being able to do what you need to do to survive can cause tremendous turmoil within the house, which ultimately can lead to even worse emotional distress than ever. You know, I hear people say all the time that money isn't everything, but I have to tell ya, money does help you with a lot of things.

However, money also doesn't create happiness. Money just escalates the person who you are already are. If you are depressed already, it can bring deeper depression into your life. Hopefully that makes sense.

- **Medications** – Depression is a side effect of many medications. For example, Accutane is a acne medicine that I used to take, and I remember reading that Accutane had been responsible for many cases of some major emotional challenges as severe as causing suicidal thoughts. They would have me come in every month and ask me several questions about my emotional health. Also, even the medicines that you see that are supposed to help with emotional challenges cause other emotional challenges, which doesn't make sense to me. Depression is a possible side effect for anxiety and insomnia drugs, including Valium and Xanax; Lopressor, prescribed to treat high blood pressure; cholesterol-lowering drugs including Lipitor; and Premarin for menopausal symptoms. Read the potential side effects when you take a new medication, and always check with your doctor to see if you might be at risk. Now, while I am not a doctor by any means, I will say I personally believe in trying to find alternative means of health care to refrain from having these horrible side effects that these prescribed medications cause.

While I am sure there may be other reasons why someone would fall into depression, I believe these 12 reasons will be a great start for anyone to possibly identify with. You may also identify with more than one, like I did. However, the main thing is to identify the root to your depression so that you can be able to better identify how to get over this. While some causes are much deeper rooted than others, and a simple snap of the fingers can't just help you get over depression, I will say at least having an idea will get you on the right track of what to do or where to seek help.

Chapter 4 :
7 Ways to Fight Depression

"Beloved, do not be surprised at the fiery trial when it comes upon you to test you, as though something strange were happening to you. But rejoice insofar as you share Christ's sufferings, that you may also rejoice and be glad when his glory is revealed. If you are insulted for the name of Christ, you are blessed, because the Spirit of glory and of God rests upon you." (1 Peter 4:12-14 ESV)

Getting over this emotional illness has been an everyday walk. It has been something that honestly, I have still had to deal with today. It's not something you just snap your fingers and all of a sudden it's completely gone. If you can fall into it one time, you can fall into it again. The key is to understand that a lot of times if we are aware of our emotions and what we are focusing our attention on, then we can truly be able to separate those feelings and turn this illness around! By the way, let me make another disclaimer: I am in no way a doctor, psychiatrist, or any of that. I am just a woman who is sharing with you my personal testimonial with a few additional things I researched. However, I do believe that if you follow these different tasks, it will help you.

So here are my seven ways to live and let go of this depression. By the way, I can't wait for you to read the personal stories of some incredible men and women who participated in sharing their stories with me. I know you are going to absolutely love them! They are toward the end of the book, and these will help you as well. I feel that a lot of times, when we can hear stories of other people that we may identify with, it is also inspirational to us as well.

1. **Get a Routine** – The first thing I would recommend is getting yourself a routine. If you have ever suffered from depression or if you are currently feeling

that weight on your shoulders, then you may experience those amazing days of doing absolutely nothing. If you are more like me, you may have even indulged in some beverages that caused you to be even lazier. I would literally lay in my bed every single day watching every single program and ignoring every single call. The day I made a decision that I didn't want depression to continue to control my life, I had to set a game plan of the things I would do to get myself out of the bed. I literally scheduled my day. I would actually schedule my month in advance. This was something I used to do anyway with my business when it was growing at its peak. I would schedule everything.

While I know I wasn't ready to go 100% back into building my business, I had to identify the things that made me happy. So to get this routine together, I first built a list of five things I liked to do outside of the house. I love the movies; I love to spend time with my puppy; I love to literally go people watch in really nice establishments—you know, those places with the "rich" and "famous"; I also liked to go to church. So what I did was schedule my days with simple things that I would do to get out of the house. Now, I will tell you, it still wasn't a quick fix. I scheduled these days, and some days I still didn't want to get out of bed; however, the more I scheduled, the more I felt compelled to just get out and see what would happen. One of the things that did always keep me excited was going to church. I then made a decision to make a deeper commitment to the church and join a group, which is another section I'll talk about in this chapter. So I started setting this routine. I would force myself to just get up and get out, and the more I did, the better I became. Please know that this was just one piece to my personal puzzle. For some of you, this could be all you need to do, but I highly doubt it.

2. **Exercise** – There are different kinds of exercises that you can do to truly help your body. One of the reasons why exercise is recommended for depression

is because when you exercise, your body releases chemicals called endorphins. These endorphins interact with the receptors in your brain that reduce your perception of pain. Endorphins also trigger positive feelings in the body, similar to that of morphine. For example, the feeling that follows a run or workout is often described as "euphoric." This is according to WebMD.com, which actually makes a lot of sense. For me, when I was consistently working out, it didn't really matter a lot in regards to the circumstances in my life; I was mostly in a great mood. I loved to do a hard workout and then calm it down with a great bit of yoga exercise as well. I promise you, this was some of the best peace I ever had in my life. A great routine I would recommend for you to do is to start off with some walking and a nice yoga routine. There are routines you can actually watch right from your phone. A good 15 to 30 minutes a day is a great start. The more that you do it, the easier it becomes and the more your body will crave a good workout, not to mention the fact that you're going to start looking better; a great combination of good eating never hurt anyone either.

3. **Watch Your Nutrition** – My nutrition was horrible. I wasn't really eating at all, and when I did eat, it consisted of something fried or some

pizza. I definitely now understand that you are what you eat. Seriously, the food I was eating was most definitely killing me slowly. I never ate anything fresh. I would drink wine every single day all through the day. This caused me to gain some additional pounds and most definitely affected my emotional state. I have to be honest; I never really personally did much research on what I could and could not eat, but one of the things I did start to do more was get more fresh foods. I had a doctor tell me that if you go to a grocery store, do your best to stay on the edge of the store with your food and very little going through the aisles. So I started to get more veggies and fruits. I started juicing more and of course drinking more water. I still am not all the way there, but I am drinking far more water than wine now. Yes, I still drink wine. I never gained a dependency on the wine as in turning into an alcoholic, but I will say I was very close to it; it was only a matter of time. Both of my parents were alcoholics. While I didn't stop drinking what I like to call my "Jesus Juice," I did make sure to pay attention to what I was consuming and also set a limit on my daily intake. If I was to exceed it, then I would have to stop drinking for a while. So my focus became more on eating healthier, fresh foods, and I did start to notice a difference in my emotional state. I would recommend also consulting with possibly a nutritionist, who can give you full meal plan with ideas designed to feed your mind, body, and soul.

4. **Sleep a Good Night's Sleep – I** promise you that one of my favorite things to do is sleep. Yes, I love myself a good night's rest, or good day's rest, or whenever I can; however, the challenge was that with building my business, there were some nights when one my favorite things to do, which was sleep, was pushed to the back. I promise you this, your body needs rest, and if you don't give your body the rest it needs, you are not letting your body rejuvenate. A good night's rest helps to regulate your mood and is linked

to learning and memory function. If you don't get enough sleep, it will absolutely increase your chances to negatively affect your mood, immune system, memory, and stress level. Your body is just like a car's engine. If you run an engine forever, it will eventually heat up. When it heats up, your immune system gets weak. When your immune system is weakened, your emotions are affected.

What I would recommend is that you want to do your best to have a "sleep schedule"—one that you can stay consistent with. According to WebMD.com, it is recommended that you sleep at least seven hours of sleep per day. I know some people who say they only need to sleep four hours per day, and unfortunately, that is a setup for a setback. Eventually your body is going to shut down if you run consistently that way. You may find yourself having difficulty concentrating and more mood problems than people that do sleep seven to nine hours. Your body needs time to rest, so don't ignore your body's need for rest.

5. **Get Social Support** – I promise you this: My life completely changed when I joined what my church calls a "starting point group," which is the same thing as a social support group. The main purpose was really to learn more about the story of Jesus and how to grow deeper

in faith. Even though this group really didn't discuss what we were dealing with on a daily basis, I found it refreshing to attend our meetings. I learned that so many of the other group members also had so many things going on, and that ultimately was the reason why they joined the group. Some were even dealing with way more challenging things than I was. This helped me a lot because I was in a group of people who really didn't know me. They didn't judge me. They didn't assume anything, because there was really no history on which to base their views of me. They just loved on me. It's really hard to explain, but this group just really did so much for me. We then extended our meetings to a Bible study, which was even more exciting. I've had a few people who have reached out to me personally about getting through depression, and to them all, I recommended finding a small group to join. I am a Christian, so I joined one with my church. I also joined a non-denominational group, and that's just my personal preference. I like to be able to be comfortable in my own skin and not worry about what I can and can't wear. I just love a laidback environment. I will tell this to anyone: This was the first step in my true recovery of getting over depression. Now, I'm pretty sure some reading this book may not necessarily agree or understand why I am in a non-denominational church, but for me, I've learned more about the Bible and, most importantly, myself than ever in my life. However, let's not get off topic; I just totally love my church and the community.

Joining a positive group of people will always be great. You can even start your own, but let me recommend that you don't create a group where you only discuss the bad things going on in your life. That will only make you feel worse. The key is to get around people that want to focus on the positive things—things that will motivate you to see that beautiful light at the end of your dark tunnel. It can be a group where you guys go out and enjoy different activities as well—anything that can get you out of the house and around some positive and encouraging people.

6. **Do Something New** – Sometimes bringing new, exciting activities into your life can absolutely change your emotions. It can be any kind of activity. For me, I would attend different "artsy" type of events. I enjoy being able to be creative, so I took a few different art classes. Also, you can do things like sculpting, dancing, and attending shows and sporting activities. Honestly, anything that is different than your norm can absolutely help in changing your state. Think about

it; it is your current activities or even lack there of that may put you in the state you are in. So changing up what you do on a regular basis can absolutely help you. You can also take time to go to a resort spa, where you can rest. Here in Georgia there is a spa that I would spend time at where you can actually go in and spend the night.

Also, something new is changing something like the route that you normally drive. If you go a certain route to work, switch it up and find a more scenic route. It's weird, but when you become accustomed to your everyday routine, it can directly affect your mood, so give yourself something new to see that can give you some new excitement.

7. **Take Responsibility** – So, honestly, I know in this book, it may seem like I take a lot of this conversation lightly because of course my personality comes out, but I want you to know that depression is no joke. It was not funny at all to me while I was actually going through it. However, I will say it wasn't serious for me until the day that Monica, my BFF, actually told me that I needed to get out of the bed. I mean, literally, my bed had become my favorite place to be. I had bags of empty food boxes all over the place. At one point, there were almost four empty bottles of wine on my

nightstand. It wasn't until then that I finally made a decision to admit that I was going through this depression and that I didn't want to deal with it anymore. I had gotten tired of the thoughts of ending it all. I was sick and tired of honestly being sick and tired. I made a true decision that I wanted get better. I knew I was going through depression, and I knew that this wasn't who I was. I also understood that I had to take back control of my state. By the way, in case you aren't sure what I mean when I say "state," I am talking about your current emotion at that time. I knew that I wanted to take back control of my state, and I knew that it needed to happen fast. The thoughts of suicide were increasing every single day. You know, to tell you the truth, the true reason why I honestly believe I didn't make that final decision to end it all was because the statistics of suicide were not positive as far as people having success in attempting to end their lives. The only way to have a 100% success rate was too dramatic for me. I can't believe I'm telling you all this, but it is so important for me to discuss. I made a decision that I was only being selfish in thoughts of suicide and that it was time to get off my pity party and get myself better. I didn't want to feel this pain anymore, and it wasn't until then that I truly was ready to take responsibility for my emotions and take my power back. I encourage you, if you are reading this book because you are personally suffering from depression, that you, too, have the ability to take your power back. I assume that if you are reading this for yourself, you have already admitted to yourself that you are troubled, but now you have to take responsibility for your state and make a decision that you want to be in control of your emotions because at the end of the day, you truly are in control.

<u>Chapter 5 :</u>
<u>Help Someone with</u>
<u>Depression</u>

"For I know the plans I have for you, declares the LORD, plans for welfare and not for evil, to give you a future and a hope." (Jeremiah 29:11 ESV)

For me, I think this chapter is one of the most important. The reason why I believe this is one of the most important is because when I did make a decision that I wanted to get help, I reached out to a few people to tell them what was going on with me, and honestly, I believe most did not know what to do with my unveiling. I guess I can get it. In most cases when you did see me in the public, I would wear a smile on my face like nothing was wrong. Nobody really knew all that was happening in my life. The only way you really knew was if you lived with me. Outside of that, yes, I'm sure some people could tell a little that I was dealing with something but not the extent that I had fallen to.

So the reason why I think this is important is because I had a friend whom I believe if I were better at responding to her, I could have helped her more. Let's be honest, when someone is troubled, in most cases, our response is to pray about it or seek a counselor or something like that. However, that was not what I wanted to hear. I didn't want to be told to just pray about it or that maybe I should do this or do that. For me, the best way to help is to just be there and support me. So with that, I have also included six different things that you can do for anyone in your life that is dealing with depression. I pray that these tips can be shared with so many so that we can better combat this very powerful emotional disease.

1. **Don't Ignore It** – The worst thing you can do is try to ignore the situation or avoid it. If your friend or loved one is clearly dealing with depression, don't ignore it. The best thing Monica could have done for me was literally tell me that I just had to get out of the bed. I know that she may have been a bit nervous to tell me that. I have such a strong personality, and she is just a soft-spoken, sweet person. So when she told me that I needed to change something, it really made me look at myself in the mirror. If you know someone is struggling with depression, don't ignore it. Tell them you see that they are dealing with something and that you are there for them.

2.   **Don't Tell Them, Just Do** – I hate when someone tells me that I should do this and do that or that we will go do this or do that. When someone is dealing with depression, you must remember in most cases they don't really care too much about what's coming. Honestly, when you are depressed, it's the one emotion that causes you to not live in the present or future. You more so living in the past. It's like a numb feeling or just blah. So for me, I didn't want to hear about what we were going to do. It's always better to just do. I remember several situations where it was just like, Taurea, let's get up and get out. Even though I went kicking and screaming, I would eventually get up and

honestly enjoy myself. Now, of course, it wasn't the cure, so when I went back home, I fell back into depression, but at least I was able to change my state, which was absolutely helpful for me.

3. **Listen** – Do your best to just listen to them without commenting. Seriously, please, no commenting. In most cases, when I did express to someone what I was going through, I really just wanted to be able to just share my feelings without a back-and-forth conversation. I just needed someone that I could just release to and let it out of my head. In some cases for those whom I reached out to, it was like they wanted to try to compete with me on conversation. I would say

something then they would say something—just back and forth—and honestly, I felt like they weren't really listening. It doesn't mean they weren't really listening, but remember, I'm in a state of being honestly selfish.

I can also relate to one of my good friends who was also going through some tough emotional challenges. She reached out to me, and I remember it like yesterday. She was in my eyes just complaining about all the challenges she was going though, and it was not really something I could truly hear. It hurt me to hear that she was going through so much pain, so I thought I was being that uplifting friend by telling her that she needed to stop talking about what she was going through. It was only making things worse, and every time we got together, it was the same story. I told her if she needed my help, she could just ask me for help. I would help her with anything. I thought I was helping her in a way. I have this saying that I know is true: "What you speak about you bring about." However, at that point, my friend didn't need a coach; she just needed a friend whom she could just release to. Unfortunately, that was the last lunch we ever had. She shut me out of her life, and I felt horrible about it. I didn't mean to make her feel worse, but that's exactly what I ended up doing.

4. **Pray for and with Them** – One of the best activities we can do for anyone is pray for them. I don't know if you are as religious as I am, and if you are not, then this part may not move you the way it moves me. For me, prayer is so powerful. Prayer has gotten me through so many things. I have had sessions where people have prayed over me, and honestly, I know that God was moving through me at these times. If I could have done anything for my friend, I could have just listened and then should have prayed. There are so many people right now dealing with so much in the world. Imagine if we all were better at praying for others more than we do for ourselves? I believe that God would

bless us with the ultimate blessings. So I ask of you, my friend, continue to pray for me and all of our brothers and sisters that may be going through emotional and/or physical sickness, and I will also continue to pray for you.

5. **Tell Them You Care** – I swear, if I could count the number of times that the thought that nobody even cared about came across my mind... I mean, seriously, I would feel like if I were no longer here, nobody would really care. I felt like maybe my desire to impact lives really wasn't as strong as I had thought. Of course, I know today that this was false. However, I will say the people in my life who absolutely blessed me the most were

those who showed little gestures of appreciation. I remember Monica brought me a card telling me how much she appreciated me. I still have that card displayed on my dining table because it really meant so much to me.

Sometimes the only thing you can really do for someone going through depression is to make sure they know that you care about them and that you value them in your life. Giving them a call or sending a text message, an email, a card, or just about anything will let them know you appreciate them. In many cases of depression, people truly just want to feel appreciated. While I am writing this, it also came to mind that maybe you are thinking, "Taurea, I hear you and all, but this isn't my fault. I didn't do anything to them, but every time I reach out to them, they seem to be irritated with me, like I'm worrying them." My answer to you is this: Remember that when you are going through depression, 9 times of 10 you are really just thinking of your situation. It's truly a selfish state in a way. Trust me when I say that in most cases, they don't mean for you to feel like they don't appreciate you reaching out as long as you aren't reaching out with judgment and/or comments but are just truly displaying your appreciation for them; trust me, they really need it. Keep on letting them know you appreciate them.

Keep on letting them know you care. This could be one of the greatest things you do for this person. I know from personal experience.

6. **Offer Help** – This is a very touchy approach to helping someone going through depression. If you remember earlier in this chapter, I thought I was offering help to my friend; however, it only came out as being judgmental in her eyes. It doesn't matter what I meant; it only matters what she felt. So when it comes to offering help, don't just make a suggestion; you be the help.

Here's an example of what I mean. If you believe your loved one should maybe reach out to an expert or a small group, which you know is my recommendation, then spend some time finding one for them. Take them to meet the leader. Maybe you can take the time to call the group and find out what they are about, and you can drive your loved one to that first meeting. Seriously, wouldn't it be worth you putting in this little bit of time to save them from the circumstances of continued depression? If I would have thought about it, I could have really done more for my friend instead of telling her to stop talking about her challenges. I mean, honestly, let's be real. The challenges she had were really a big deal, and it wasn't like ignoring them would cause them to go away. She needed a solution. She needed help. I could have been that true friend and decided, okay, this is what we are going to do.

Another example I can give you is my friend Stacii Jae, who has just been an incredible asset to my life. In fact, I like to call her the number one action taker. So while trying to really decide the path in which I needed to move forward on in regards to business, I was allowing my situation to really affect my attitude toward the actions that I needed to take. I remember her calling me up with a game plan that she had designed all to help me get things going to another level. Not only was it great information but it also felt really good. Stacii girl, I don't even know if I ever told you how much I appreciate you for that, but just in case I never did, I wanted to leave it forever in this book and tell you THANK YOU. God doesn't always bless you with people in your life like that who can really help get you out of the funk that you are in. The great thing is we really do work well together in helping each other with ideas and goals.

You may say to yourself, this sounds great and all, but what if I don't know how to help? Sometimes helping can be just as simple as getting them to go to a group meeting with you or finding someone or something that can help them get their mind off things. I have been blessed with some incredible friends who have at times done just that. These friends include my good friend who I have talked about a lot, Monica Wilkerson. The other friends I would like to mention include Diana Perez, Demi Davis, Jannell Speight, and Dr. Sharon Wilborn. Ladies, if I never told you thank you, thank you for just being incredibly visionary women. I so appreciate you all for always being in my life and not letting me stay where I was. There are so many other friends that I have that have also been there for me in different ways. If I left out anyone I just want you to know I do appreciate you for who you are. There are so many that I could name but I would be here all day thinking. What's crazy, is at the time of my depression, I felt like I had nobody.

Chapter 6 :
Stories of Survivors

"I waited patiently for the LORD; he inclined to me and heard my cry. He drew me up from the pit of destruction, out of the miry bog, and set my feet upon a rock, making my steps secure. He put a new song in my mouth, a song of praise to our God. Many will see and fear, and put their trust in the LORD." (Psalm 40:1-3 ESV)

From Panic & Anxiety Attacks

My name is Tracee Randall, and I am grateful to be a survivor of depression. I have been depressed for as long as I can remember. The main reason for my depression was that my mom had very low self-esteem issues. As I watched her compare herself to models in fashion magazines and on TV, I began to do the same. We both dieted endlessly, and I fought bouts of anorexia and bulimia. She had no idea that her own issues were causing me to hate everything about myself. More than anything, I hated looking in the mirror.

By the time I was 43, I was having such panic and anxiety attacks that I rarely left my home. I didn't want to wake up in the morning, and all I wanted to do was go back to bed at night—and then I could not sleep.

The only thing that kept me on this side of suicide during that time was my church and my love for my family. God's Word and His promises inspired me to continue living. But even then my panic attacks would cripple me, and although by this time I had become a master at hiding it, I did my best to avoid people.

I was introduced to a nutritional product when I was 47 years old that changed everything. As I felt better and had more energy, my depression began to lift. After years of depriving my body of nutrients through dieting, I was suddenly feeling amazing. I began to leave my house and meet people. Although I still had many fears, I was *encouraged* to teach others about the product and to share my testimony.

I met a woman who was about 10 years older than me. She began to speak greatness over me. I began to learn about the power of our WORDS and THOUGHTS. I began to speak WORDS of affirmation over MYSELF and listen to positive teachings by Jim Rohn and others. Slowly, I began to see myself differently. I began to LIKE ME for the first time, and my fear of people began to subside.

As I began to see myself as God sees me, slowly my thoughts about myself began to change. As I began to accept my own inner beauty, my eyes were opened, and suddenly my world was filled with a joy that is unexplainable.

In 2014 I began to write. I had not written in a journal since 1984. I had laid down my writing to raise children and to build businesses, but one night I began writing about our 30th wedding anniversary, and I titled it "I Got Married in the Hospital" and posted it on Facebook. The next morning there were hundreds of posts asking for more. My love for writing was rekindled! Since then I have been published in several women's magazines, and I am speaking to women across the country about these issues—how I overcame self-hate and food addiction to be the woman that God always intended me to be!

I am beautiful. I am amazing. I am a child of God. I am loved, and I love. I am walking into my destiny in #MiracleTerritory and according to #GodsPlan.

I assumed he was happy because he had everything....

My name is Angie Renee', and my cousin, Greg, suffered from depression. We were very close and were raised as if we were brother and sister. We were only seven months apart and did absolutely everything together. I always assumed that he was so happy because not only did he always smile, but he had everything! Growing up, I always found myself admiring him because he seemed to get everything that he wanted. Once we got older, I moved to Atlanta. A few years later, he followed suit because we were just that close. He had his own condo, and I was living with a roommate at the time. He showed absolutely no signs of depression. He was still the same old Greg whom I loved and was always very fond of. I remember getting a call from my aunt that he had passed. I couldn't believe it. My heart stopped, and the tears started to flow uncontrollably. I felt like if only I had called him the night before to go out to dinner with me, he would still be here. It has been nine years, and it still doesn't seem real to me. He had so much going for him: a beautiful fiancée, a nice condo, a hot car, and was recently promoted at his job. How could he have been depressed? I know, I asked myself the same thing. The truth is, many people hide behind masks and deal with issues that none of us know about. I found out later after his death that he always felt different because of being biracial. I knew nothing about this. I also found out that he would cry a lot when he was alone and didn't understand why. For years I felt guilty and wondered, if I had paid more attention to him, would he still be here? Depression is something that we don't talk about much in the black community. We say clichés like "Just pray about it" and "It isn't that bad. You'll be fine." We can no longer ignore this topic, and we definitely can't blow it off as if it isn't that serious. It is VERY serious! We must do our part to pay more attention and listen to our loved ones when they are hurting. We must get them the proper help they need so we can become a healthier and happier community. Even if you or no one you know personally has suffered from depression, please think about those that may come after you. For each one must teach one.

The best medicine is to be around positive, empowering people.

Marisa was diagnosed with Multiple Sclerosis, and the nature of this challenge causes her to be mindful of her mental and physical state more often than most. She lives alone, and very few people, including her family, even check on her. If she was not a strong-willed and determined woman, depression could easily dictate her everyday life. Living with the challenges of a chronic

119

disease can cause someone to fall in and out of depression.

Whenever she is not having a good day, meaning she feels weak, is experiencing pain, etc., Marisa knows she should not subject herself to any negativity or any undue stress. She does not watch TV and does not go out often. The latter has become a behavior she must overcome if she wants to be successful in her current business venture. The reality is no one has total control over these triggers. Managing her environment and paying close attention to her body enables her to keep depression at bay most of the time. When depression does try to raise up, she calls on her best friend, Sebastian. He reminds her, "As long as you do not have a Post-it on your front door from God that says He cannot help you anymore, you will be just fine." Sebastian knows Marisa better than anyone else, so he can easily determine when there may be an issue brewing and usually knows exactly what to say to her to lift her spirits.

Marisa has oftentimes said MS is her barometer to let her know when something is not right. Actually, it is a blessing because she can detect any changes in her state of mind based on how it is manifested in her body. Half the battle is already won once you know where you are headed. Now you know you have to take action to get yourself back on track.

She has set some goals and dreams that will enable her to have a better quality of life, where even the simple things are no longer so challenging for her to accomplish. Marisa does not concern herself about the lack of support from some family members.

Marisa is a positive and focused person. She does not get involved in the issues of others unless called upon, and she is a very good listener. She knows the frustration of trying to tell your story while the other person is so focused on themselves that they really make matters worse without realizing it or even caring. This is probably what has caused her to be a "loner." She now realizes the best medicine for a troubled heart is to be surrounded by positive, empowering people. Thankfully, her depression has never reached the level where she has considered taking her own life.

We all face various events in our lives that cause us to ask "WHY?" The key is to know yourself and keep in tune with any changes in your overall behavior.

There is nothing wrong in saying I need help.

When we talked about depression, I think it was the first time I had admitted to anyone outside of my family or a counselor that I had ever been depressed. I used to say I was stressed out, but in reality, I was depressed. Two times the sadness got to the point where I said, "I need help." Both times I realized that I was just kind of going through the motions. I continued to work. I engaged with patients, I smiled, and I even laughed...while I was at work. But when I came home, it was another story.

I felt so alone, yet I wouldn't reach out for fear of judgment. What would they think? What would they say? Many nights I sat on the couch, watching television, counting the hours before it was an acceptable time to go to sleep. I tried to numb the pain with alcohol and fill the void with food. I didn't call my mom, because she could always hear it in my voice, no matter how much I tried to mask it. I didn't want to have to lie or put on the false smile in response to her question, "What's the matter, Baby?"

Working was good for me because I was forced to be around people. Money rolled in because I worked all the time to avoid myself, to avoid going home and being alone.

At the time, I blamed the man I had dated for many years, the one who made all of these promises but never came through. I won't go into details, but you could not make this stuff up even if you were writing it for a soap opera.

As a healthcare provider, the subject of depression can be tricky. We don't want any diagnoses of mental illness on our records, so we suffer in silence. As an African-American, there is a stigma against seeking counsel outside of church and girlfriends. The unspoken rule is that you have to be strong, which means don't cry, and keep it moving. If we don't take care of ourselves, how can we take care of others?

I have learned that there is nothing wrong with saying, "I need help," and crying is cleansing. A young lady asked me once, "Where do you think cancer comes from?" I believe it sometimes comes from holding things in that must be released. Because I touched on it here, I will say that I also believe that addiction comes from trying to numb pain and distract ourselves to fill a void.

The biggest piece of advice I would give to anyone going through this is to find someone you trust and confide in them. If you fear judgment from your friends/family, seek counsel. Some churches have licensed counselors on staff for free. If you are a

126

healthcare provider in a large organization, find your Employee Assistance Program. They usually provide stress counseling for free.

I had to pretty much press the restart button.

My name is Carlos L. Brown, and I am a survivor of depression. At the time, I was a husband and a father, and some people knew I was going through this health challenge.

I believe the main reason for my depression was that at the time, I was in the military, going on deployments, and away from the family. While away, my ex was cheating on me, and the person had the nerve to send me a message on social media to tell me about it.

At the time of my depression, I was not able to sleep comfortably; I was not speaking to everyone. And if I did speak to someone, I would have an attitude. I also didn't eat healthy.

It wasn't until my contract ended in the Navy in 2012 that I decided to work on the problem. I was home more but unemployed at the same time. I tried to work it out with my ex, but she felt without me being in the Navy, I wasn't useful anymore. So I started working on getting through this illness of depression.

As I was going through the separation, I had to pretty much press the restart button and move back in with my mother. I had the support of God, my family, and also some close friends. Now that I am out of that situation, I have felt better than I ever felt before. I get text messages from time to time with a sob story. I pay that no mind, because if it's not about my kids, it's not important to me.

If I could share one thing with anyone who is going through depression, I would tell them never to give up and to constantly pray. Prayers will get answered, and the grass is greener on the other side.

I've been working on finding me.

My name is LaWonda, and not only am I a mother, a wife, and a medical assistant but I'm a survivor of depression. For me, I realized I was depressed when my youngest son was about three months old. I guess I always had known I was depressed, but I tried to ignore it. My husband knew something was wrong but didn't really understand, and the doctor I work for knew I was dealing with depression after I finally broke down in his office. I believe the main reason for my depression was that I was carrying everyone else's cross, burdens, and responsibilities. My husband and I both were working and living paycheck to paycheck, having up to 10 people living with us, and trying to make things work off a two-income home—from having cars repossessed, lights being shut off, and going to food pantries for food to feed us all. Not only that but we were taking on the responsibility of getting custody of two nieces and a nephew. At the time of my depression, I would distance myself from any and everyone. I had to force myself out of the bed in the mornings for work, but being at work helped me somewhat because it was some form of peace. Sometimes I would lock myself in the restroom and just sit in silence to get some peace and quiet. I found myself getting mad at my husband and kids for no reason. I felt alone and abandoned, shut off from the world. My heart ached, but I didn't know what to do. It wasn't until the thought of going to bed and never waking up crossed my mind that it hit me that I had to take a step towards getting through this illness. The thought of my husband being alone and my kids not having their mother broke my heart. As I was going through my illness, I had my husband's support and support from people I work with. I'm still dealing with depression, but I found a church home, and I love to sing (not that I'm a good singer); it helped, and I'm also working on talking about my feelings and not holding it all in. I've been working on finding me. If I could share one thing with anyone that is going through depression I would tell them to find a support group, don't give up, and PRAY.

I asked God to take away this illness.

I believe the main reason for my depression was that I was five months pregnant, and my daughter's dad tried to find any reason to put me out. He came up with a crazy one at that, so at five months pregnant, I was put out of my home. I didn't want anyone to know, so I would go to work some days, get a hotel room after work, and some days go to my cousin's house. I would call him throughout the day, and he wouldn't answer my calls. At the time of my depression, I would go to work and go stay with my cousin; it wasn't until I was seven months pregnant that I explained to my mom what was going on in my life, and that helped me take a step with getting help with this illness. As I was getting through this, I had the support of my mom and cousin. To this day, I'm still battling with depression. Sometimes I don't know if I'm coming or going. I want to be successful so bad; it's about to drive me crazy. I get so down and out because I don't know if the moves I'm making are the right moves, not to mention I'm a single parent in the process of trying to succeed. I plan on getting help soon. I pray and ask God to take this illness away because I need to be here for my daughter.

Her baby changed her life for the better.

Her story started seven years ago. She was an outgoing person but found herself being alone and no longer socializing with friends. The days seemed to be longer and longer. She had no clue what happened to her, but she realized she was fighting depression. Her mother died suddenly, and the guilt was all over her. She was feeling too sick to attend her mother's funeral. She was pregnant at the time, and it was said it was a mistake to be in that position and that it could kill her. Her doctor said that she would end up having a stroke and even asked if she wanted to get an abortion. The world was dark, and she felt she had no hope. Sometimes she felt better if the pain would go away, not just the physical pain but the inner pain. The pain of feeling she had no self worth. The pain of feeling like giving up on life. She couldn't handle the stress of her life. Several months later a beautiful baby was born; she held him and felt a sense of peace. She was so glad that he wasn't a victim of abortion, because now he's a joy in her life. He allowed her faith in Christ to open up. She now had a testimony on how being depressed will put you in a dark life; the enemy wants to keep people in bondage for decisions they make in life and lead them to believe that killing yourself is the answer. This baby changed her life, and he broke the hold of the enemy. He is a gift from God who reminds her that God is there for us. We just have to believe and trust him with our lives.

<u>I never lost faith.</u>

My name is Michael Brown, and to be honest, I never looked at what I was going through as depression, although someone else may call it that. I was 16, and life wasn't horrible, but things were not that great either, in my mind. No one knew of my internal challenges or feelings because I didn't feel anyone would care or remotely come close to understanding.

In my eyes, my father was showing far more love and affection to my younger brother, who he biologically wasn't connected to. Words like "I love you" or even "I'm proud of you" were demonstrated to my brother but not me as far as I was aware of. I was constantly ridiculed for not growing up fast enough to think for myself and my brother when I was watching him; I got in trouble regularly for things he did since I was the oldest. This started when I was nine.

School was probably one of the worst places for me to be. Constant teasing, mocking, and a small degree of bullying were part of my life, although I was the type to continue on like there was no issue. I believed I was able to shake it all off. The biggest contributor was the fact that I was a father to a two-year-old son. The news when he was born didn't hit my family so well. I had family who said some very mean things about him not being mine and even things that would make a person think I was having sex with a lot of people because I had a child.

One day every pain caught up to me. I came home from school and went into the kitchen. I grabbed one of the sharpest knives we owned and lunged it towards my stomach. As if in a movie, literally, flashes of my son flooded my mind. Before the knife got to my skin, I stopped. I let go of the knife and dropped to my knees, crying. I had a purpose for being here that was bigger than me. I was a father, and he was going to need me.

No one knew of this, and to this day, many still don't. My spiritual connection increased dramatically, and I knew that was all I needed to endure and keep moving.

If I could share one piece of advice for anyone going through a moment of deep despair, I would say you are not truly alone. In a world where so many things are happening, it's easy to feel like a speck surrounded by others that may not seem to care what is going on with you. But there is a force of power that goes beyond all the people on the planet. That force showed me my son is why I'm important. I never lost faith. You can't lose it either.

Meditation and prayer helped her.

She dealt with depression from the time she was a child. She goes back that far because she can remember creating a fantasy world by mentally placing herself in another country and another time. When this did not work, she had thoughts of killing herself. This continued off and on (more on than off) from the age of five until early midlife. She sought help from psychologists to no avail. Depression led to her being hospitalized for a period. This depression came from sexual child abuse. It was not until much later in life that she discovered she gained the most help from meditation and prayer. Through these, she was able to work on changing her mindset. She discovered it was not what happened to her but how she looked at what happened to her.

Seek Help and Rely on God's Power

My name is Natasha Roach, and I am a survivor of depression. At the time of my depression, I was a young single woman working as a teacher and going to school to complete a Master's degree. No one knew I was going through this health challenge.

For me, I believe the main reason for my depression was not knowing how to handle the passing of my childhood friend. We were so close, and for her to pass so suddenly, and at such a young age, it was difficult for me to cope with. Replaying many of the events that happened prior to the death of my friend made the situation worse. During one of her last birthdays, we had our first and only dispute in our entire friendship. Even though we reconciled our differences shortly after the incident, I selfishly vowed never to celebrate my birthday out of fear that something like this would happen again. The woeful thing about my decision was that my friend passed before my next birthday.

At the time of my depression, I would work like crazy, staying busy but not efficient. My effectiveness at work had diminished, I missed major projects for school, causing my GPA to drop drastically, and I exercised aggressively for six days a week. I thought that I was functioning normally, but I didn't realize that I had begun to isolate myself, and other things began to deteriorate as well.

It wasn't until my health forced me to go to the doctor that I was able to take a step toward getting through this illness. My doctor told me that I was suffering from post-traumatic stress and had a failing digestive system, and she informed me that I was threatening the need for medication. Instead, my doctor told me to seek my Primary Physician for healing. My doctor highlighted a few scriptures and told me to follow up with her later.

As I was getting through this, I prayerfully sought God for counsel, strength, and peace. While I had family and friends that were always praying for me, I did this on my own. Over time, God showed me how to overcome by focusing on what He wanted me to learn not only from her passing but from her life.

I am no longer dealing with this issue. I celebrate her life as well as my own!

If I could share one thing with anyone that is going through depression, I would tell them to seek help and to rely on God's power. His grace is sufficient, and His strength is made perfect in our weakness.

Take Action Today

"Humble yourselves, therefore, under the mighty hand of God so that at the proper time he may exalt you, casting all your anxieties on him, because he cares for you." (1 Peter 5:6-7 ESV)

Now that you have read this book through to the end and you've read the incredible stories of survivors, the next key to this is to take action, regardless of which side of the fence you are on. You may be suffering from depression or you may know or even suspect someone who is; the key is to take action. If no action is taken, there can be no resolution to this terrible disease. I personally would love to hear from you. I want to be able to share with the world that regardless of what nationality you are, it is okay to be where you are. We can work together to get through this.

There are so many of our brothers and sisters that are living with this disease, and it won't change unless we remove the perception and judgment of depression. Let's take action together on getting through this! Contact me today to learn more about what we are doing to overcome this disease. To do so, simply go to www.TaureaAvant.com/depression today and send me a message. I so look forward to this movement helping women and men in mind, body, and soul.

Conclusion

"Blessed is the one whose transgression is forgiven, whose sin is covered." (Psalm 32:1 ESV)

First of all, from the bottom of my heart, I just want to say THANK YOU SO MUCH for supporting this book! This book means so much to me, and I pray that if you are suffering or you know someone that is suffering from this horrible mental disease, you were able to learn more about where depression comes from and what we can do to combat it. One of the things that I know I have been called here to do is to impact the lives of people all over the world, and I know for that to happen, I can't do it alone. So with that said, I want to invite you to join me in becoming a part of the Vision Team. Together we can impact more lives in mind, body, and soul.

One of the things that I am doing in regards to this book is that for every book ordered, a small portion of the proceeds will be donated to a non-profit that specifically focuses on getting rid of depression and increasing happiness. For more information on that, be sure to contact me via my website. As part of the Vision Team, you can also help to get the word out about this book. Not only will you be helping the person that reads the book but you will also be helping to bring more awareness to depression and how we can help combat it one person at a time. If you want to be a part of the Vision Team, please visit my website at www.TaureaAvant.com/VisionTeam for more information.

There are some incredible benefits that align with being a part of the Vision Team as well, so just check out the site for the full details. I again want to thank you so much for your support of this book, and I pray that it was incredible for you. Please don't hesitate to shoot me a testimonial as well. My email is Taurea@taureaavant.com.

With love, honor, and humility, I want you to know I appreciate you! God bless!

About the Author

"When the righteous cry for help, the LORD hears and delivers them out of all their troubles." (Psalm 34:17 ESV)

Taurea Vision Avant started off in life with the vision of the American Dream: going to college, getting good grades, graduating, and then going off to work in Corporate America. Unfortunately, after she graduated with a bachelor's degree in computer science from Hampton University, she went from temp job to temp job to temp job. It didn't look like her dream of landing a career job in her degree was going to happen. Finally, she landed a small salaried job as a database administrator—which is just a fancy name for data entry. Even with the salaried job, she still lived paycheck to paycheck, barely making it. Can you relate?

Then the turning point in Taurea's life happened. It's what you call a "paradigm shift." (A lot of us have major turning points that will require a major shift to take place. When will your shift occur, or has it already?)

Her father, her hero, her last living parent, was diagnosed with stage 4 lung cancer in October of 2006. Her mother had passed away when she was just 12 years old due to cirrhosis of the liver, so this news totally turned her life upside down. She found herself in a place of loneliness and completely lost. She had to watch her father go through this disease and ultimately be defeated. One thing that stayed with her was this thought: Did her father seize the opportunity to do everything he wanted in life? Did he make excuses for why he couldn't do something like so many of us do? Did he lose his will to dream? She vowed from then on to not let this happen to her.

She moved to Atlanta, Ga., in August of 2007 in hopes of starting her own business in multimedia. Unfortunately, long story short, it failed. She had invested $40,000 into the business, and it turned into her making $800 in 2008. However, "We know that the most successful people in the world have failed the most on their journey to success," so she never let that hold her back. Most of us would have given up. If it weren't for failing, we wouldn't know of Henry Ford, Bill Gates, Walt Disney, Albert Einstein, Socrates, Oprah Winfrey, or Michael Jordan...JUST TO NAME A FEW!

In 2009 Taurea launched her business in direct sales, and within six months, she was able to earn over six figures in the industry. She currently holds the top rank in her current company and is in the top 1% of income earners in her industry. She is also a self-published author, co-authoring *The Golden Rule for Making Money*. She fully wrote *A Vision to Freedom...How to Truly Live the Life of Your Dreams* and *Fear – 10 Steps to Letting Go of Your Fears which is now being sold through here website www.TaureaAvant.com as well as Amazon & Barnes and Noble.* She also runs two networking groups: one for business owners and the other for women, which will soon be expanding.

Today, Taurea has been able to generate multiple streams of income, but her true passion is being able to empower women and men all over the world. Her true mission in life is to impact the lives of 10,000,000 men and women around the world.

She believes that in life, "People don't remember you for the clothes you wore, the cars you drove, or the jewelry you owned. They only remember you for the impact that you had on other people's lives." That is her true mission in life!

DEPRESSION

Enhanced Audiobook Also Available

Take the next step in implementing *DEPRESSION ~ 7 Ways to Live and Let Go*. Read by Taurea Avant, this inspiring audiobook includes additional anecdotes and success strategies from some of today's greatest achievers. This special-edition version will motivate you to move forward in growing and going to a better point in your life.

More on Taurea Avant

To have Taurea Vision Avant speak to your organization about the principles found in *A Vision to Freedom, Fear, Depression* or other success insights, e-mail speaker@showyousuccess.com.

Taurea also speaks on additional topics including:

- Book Writing (How-to)
- Public Speaking (How-to)
- Social Media
- Branding & Web Design

Follow Taurea V Avant on Social Media

Twitter.com/VisionAvant
Instagram.com/VisionAvant
Linkedin/in/VisionAvant
Facebook.com/VisionAvant
Periscope – VisionAvant

Make sure to join Taurea's visionary circle today to
stay up to date on the latest with Taurea:
www.TheVisionaryCircle.com

DEPRESSION ~ Live & Let Go!

Have you downloaded Taurea's app yet?

Search for Vision Avant on Apple Store or Play Store

Book Recommendations

I wanted to recommend other books that include some by my incredible supporters and some books that I believe would be great additions to this book.

The first set of books I have included, are books I have personally read that I believe will be a great addition to my book.

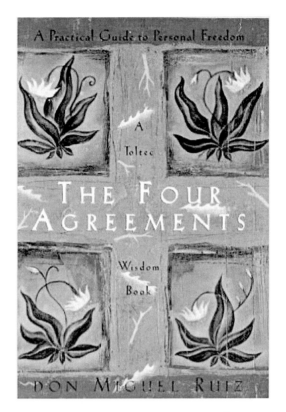

"The Four Agreements"
By
Don Miguel Ruiz

"*The Power of Now*"
by
Eckhart Tolle

"The Secret"
by
Rhonda Byrne

"The Power"
by
Rhonda Byrne

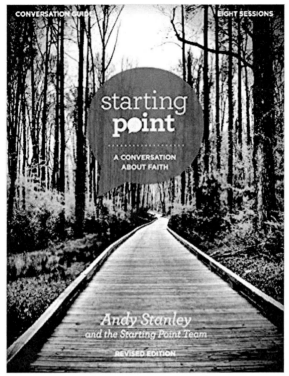

"Starting Point"
By
Andy Stanley

These books are books from some incredible visionaries who were absolutely major contributors to the production of this book. I most definitely recommend you support them and get their books as well.

"Our Story"

James & Natasha Roach
MrandMrsRoach.com

"Unstoppable Success"
TaVona Denise
TaVonaDenise.com

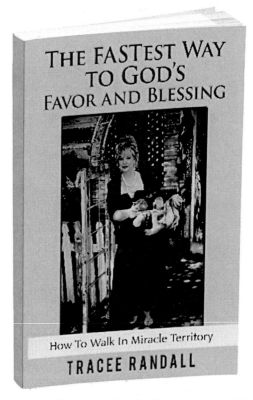

"The Fastest Way to God's Favor and Blessing"
Tracee Randall
TraceeRandall.com

"20 Beautiful Women"
Angie Renee'
www.AngieRenee.com

DEPRESSION ~ Live & Let Go!